Younger • Geertgen tot Sint Jans • **Jean-Baptiste-Camille Corot** • Camille Pissarro • **René Magritte** • Jan Jansz. Treck • **Henri Matisse** • Pierre-Étienne-Théodore Rousseau • Eugène Boudin • Meindert Hobbema • Gerrit Berckheyde • **Canaletto** • Ch'iu Ying • Hendrick ter Brugghen • **Marc Chagall** • Carlo Crivelli • Antonello da Messina • Frans Hals • Bartolomé Esteban Murillo • Jan Gossaert • Willem Van de Velde • **Joseph Mallord William Turner** • Henri Rousseau • Giacomo Balla • Victor Vasarely • Jan Vermeer • Piero della Francesca • **Titian** • Charles Demuth • **Sir Joshua Reynolds** • Jean-Siméon Chardin • Caspar David Friedrich • Francesco di Antonio • Quentin Massys • Rogier Van der Weyden • **Paul Cézanne** • Jean Dubuffet • Michael Craig-Martin • **Robert Rauschenberg** • Duccio di Buoninsegna • Anonymous

DISNEP

Looking at Paintings

An Introduction to Fine Art for Young People

Erika Langmuir & Ruth Thomson

BUNKER HILL PUBLISHING

BOSTON

About this book

This book is for children. Like the founders of the National Gallery, and all of us who work here now, it is dedicated to the certainty that great paintings enhance life and can be enjoyed by everyone. And since all children enjoy making pictures, they, above all, deserve to be introduced to some of the greatest ever made.

In common with the best guides, this one leads from the familiar to the unfamiliar, giving confidence and pleasure along the way. Perhaps no one is better known, or gives more pleasure to millions of children and adults, than Mickey Mouse and his friends. But that is not the only reason why we are glad to see them in the National Gallery. Disney cartoons have always brilliantly exploited the pictorial inventions of the old masters, and so Mickey, created only in 1928, seems happily at home throughout the whole of Western art, from cave painting to Leonardo da Vinci, Titian and Monet. I, for one, believe that he helped create Mona Lisa's smile. Following Mickey's footsteps in the cartoon strips alternating here with the main text, his fans will also learn - and I suspect never forget - how eggs and gold coins were once used in pictures, the subjects favored by seventeenth-century Dutch artists, or the Impressionists' problems in painting outdoors.

More important than these glimpses of the past is the book's message that the best pictures are forever. Like photographs, posters and postcards, cartoons or moving pictures on the screen, the paintings in galleries and museums, however old and rare, are part of today's present. They are ours for the looking and Looking at Paintings is fun.

Neil MacGregor

Neil MacGregor, Director
National Gallery, London, 1986-200

A word from Disney HAND

We at DisneyHand, worldwide outreach for The Walt Disney Company, are pleased to share with you this copy of Disney's Looking at Paintings. This wonderful volume from Disney Publishing Worldwide enlists a great friend of children everywhere – Mickey Mouse – to help kids discover the extraordinary experience of visiting the National Gallery and explore many vibrant works of art, each with its own fascinating story to tell. This gift is part of our commitment to imagination and learning as exemplified by the DisneyHand Teacher Awards, honoring creativity in teaching. We hope that it will be a useful tool to help you engage young people in creative ways of looking at the world around them.

Disney's Looking at Paintings also strives to make children aware that the National Gallery's paintings, like all great works of art, are part of a creative continuum. The artists were influenced by artists before them and, in turn, they influence artists today. DisneyHand is dedicated to making the dreams of families and children a reality through public service initiatives, community outreach and volunteerism in the areas of learning, compassion, the arts and the environment. We salute you, in turn, for your dedication to the children with whom you work; they are the artists and creative visionaries of the future, and their success is made possible by the passion you bring to your work each and every day.

Best wishes from your friends at . . .

Disney Publishing Worldwide

Disney HAND
Worldwide Outreach for The Walt Disney Company

For more information, please visit us at www.DisneyHand.com.

Contents

Meeting Pictures

People have always made pictures – you've surely done it yourself – and most of us like to look at them. Pictures are music for the eyes. Shapes, colors and lines sing and dance to the picture-maker's tune.

But many people are shy of paintings made by full-time, professional artists. They feel they ought to have special knowledge to enjoy the kind of pictures that probably cost a lot of money, or were painted a long time ago and are now shown in museums or galleries.

Yet any viewer can get pleasure from pictures – whether portraits, landscapes, still lifes, pictures that tell a story or just show lines, shapes and colors. Some are easy to understand and like at first sight. Others take longer. You need to ask

them questions to get to know them: they may then turn out to be the most interesting.

When you first meet people, you can see what they look like and you usually know what to ask to find out more about them. The same is true of pictures. First impressions – their size, shape and colors – are a good place to start; but you may not know how to go on from there. This book suggests questions you can ask of all pictures, but especially Western paintings, to find out more about them. It should give you the confidence to enter into conversation with them, so that you enjoy spending time in their company.

Chapter 1

Why do People want Pictures?

PICTURES ARE EVERYWHERE. What sort of pictures do you have in your room? Perhaps there is a poster of someone you like, a school photograph, postcards to remind you of a vacation or a picture you have painted yourself. Comics and books tell stories in pictures. Food packagings have pictures to tell you what's inside them. Pictures on greetings cards celebrate special days or events.

Take a look around

Notice how many different kinds
of pictures you see the next time
you go out. There are huge
billboards with advertisements,
posters stuck on fences and
photographs in shop windows.
There are pictures at stations,
in airports and on the sides
of buses.

Picture this

Today it is easy to print thousands of copies of a picture or to send an image to millions of homes at once. But imagine living with no cameras or TV, no computers or printers. Imagine a world without books, magazines and comics or color posters, postcards or advertisements.

One of a kind

Before any of these things existed, pictures were far rarer and more precious. As a rule, artists in Europe would paint a picture to hang in a church, a town hall or the palace of a king. People had to travel especially to see it.

For a long time, artists did not paint whatever they felt like painting. Royal families and wealthy people told artists what they wanted in their pictures.

How do I look?

In a world without cameras, a painted portrait was the only way of recording what someone looked like. Artists might be asked to paint a good likeness of their subjects or to make them seem more attractive or grander than they really were. People often dressed in special clothes and were shown with objects that tell you something about them. Portraits were expensive. Only the wealthy could afford them.

Self Portrait in a Straw Hat
after 1782

Elizabeth Louise Vigée Le Brun

Portrait of a Gentleman
probably about 1555–60

Giovanni Battista Moroni

Las Meninas 1656 **Diego Velázquez**

The artist

The princess,
the Infanta
Margarita

Part of the family

European royal families sometimes employed
an artist to work exclusively for them, to paint
portraits of themselves and their courtiers.
Velázquez was court painter to the king of Spain
for over thirty years. He became a close friend
of the king and included himself in this picture
as part of the royal household.

The king
and queen

Mr and Mrs
William Hallett
('The Morning Walk')
1785

Thomas
Gainsborough

A special event

People also asked artists to paint
pictures recording a special event.
This double portrait shows a newly-
married couple, dressed in their
best clothes, setting out on their
walk through life together. The
artist has also included their
favorite pet, a white Spitz dog.

Detail

A face in the crowd

Sometimes people wanted a group portrait to celebrate an important event or to show they were all members of an organization. These were rather like a school or team photo.

The Swearing of the Oath of Ratification of the Treaty of Münster 1648

Gerard ter Borch

The people in this picture have been lined up in rows, so most of them are clearly visible. The artist grouped the figures first. Each head was painted from life, so every individual could be easily recognised.

Details

The Emperor Napoleon I
1815

Emile-Jean-Horace Vernet

Heroes

At other times, people wanted portraits *not* of someone they knew, but of someone they admired – their hero.

Napoleon was a famous general, who became emperor of France. Admirers hung his portrait in their houses, just as you might pin up a poster of your favorite singer or a famous athlete.

Saint George and the Dragon
1889–90
Gustave Moreau

Looking like a hero

A portrait may flatter a person to make him look like a hero. In this huge portrait (*right*), King Charles I of England is shown dressed in armor, sitting calmly on his great horse. He seems powerful and ready to fight, just like his own hero, Saint George, who is said to have killed a fiery dragon (*above*). In fact, Charles was a very small man, and he later lost his kingdom – and his head!

Equestrian Portrait of Charles I
about 1637–8
Anthony van Dyck

Teaching by example

Many artists have painted scenes of everyday activities. These might contain a message about how people should behave (*below*). Parents could use them as good examples for their children.

The Courtyard of a House in Delft 1658

Pieter de Hooch

A Woman scraping Parsnips, with a Child standing by her 1655

Nicolaes Maes

Don't be so greedy

Pictures can also poke fun at mean, wicked or silly behaviour. The picture above mocks the greediness of these two men.

An aid to prayer

Some Christians like pictures of holy figures (*right*). This picture of the Virgin Mary might inspire them to spend quiet time in prayer.

Beach Scene
probably 1868–77

Hilaire-Germain-Edgar Degas

Ubbergen Castle
about 1655

Aelbert Cuyp

Painting vacations

Artists wanted to record real places they saw on their travels. They painted views of famous sights, striking buildings or landscapes as reminders of their visits, just as you might take vacation snapshots or buy picture postcards.

A Wall in Naples
about 1782

Thomas Jones

View of the Forum in Rome
1814

Christoffer Wilhelm Eckersberg

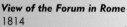

Lavacourt under Snow
about 1878–81

Claude-Oscar Monet

Fact and fantasy

The kneeling man in this picture (*right*) is a portrait of a real person, who paid to be shown praying at the feet of Saint Michael. But the artist did not know what Saint Michael looked like, so he had to use his imagination. He also invented a devil – part snake, part bird and part dragon (*below*) and imagined a reflection of the Heavenly City on Saint Michael's breastplate (*right*).

Details

Saint Michael triumphant over the Devil with the Donor Antonio Juan about 1468

Bartolomé Bermejo

Picture stories

Pictures are a good way to make stories come alive.

European artists painted Bible stories or stories about Christian saints, such as Saint Francis, who tamed a wolf (*right*). These hung in churches or in people's homes.

The Legend of the Wolf of Gubbio
1437–44   **Sassetta**

Perseus turning Phineas and his Followers to Stone
early 1680s   **Luca Giordano**

Guernica 1937 **Pablo Picasso**

An inspiring tale

Artists have also been inspired to paint ancient Greek or Roman myths. They often illustrated a dramatic part of the story, like this moment (*left*): Perseus holds up Medusa's head to turn enemy intruders at his wedding to stone.

Telling pictures

Pictures may also be inspired by real events. Before photography, artists were the people who recorded accidents, natural disasters and war.

By showing the victims of twentieth-century warfare, in this enormous picture (*above*), Picasso was able to express his horror at the suffering of innocent people.

Painted only in black, white and gray, it resembles a front-page newspaper photograph.

Showing off

Kings and princes wanted to
show off their wealth and power.
They asked artists to paint huge
pictures for rooms in their palaces.

The picture below is one of three painted
for the walls of a room in a palace in Italy.
It celebrates a real victory in battle, but
looks more like a frozen dance of richly
dressed knights on fairground horses.
Can you see any blood?

The Battle of San Romano probably about 1450–60   **Paolo Uccello**

**Flowers in a
Terracotta Vase**
1736
Jan van Huysum

Decorating the walls

Pictures may be painted purely for decoration. It became fashionable, especially in Holland, to hang paintings of fruit and flowers in the home.

Some artists specialized in detailed still lifes. This picture is so realistic you can almost smell the flowers, taste the fruits and hear insects buzzing.

MICKEY DISCOVERS CAVE PAINTINGS

BETWEEN 17,000 AND 12,000 YEARS AGO, WHEN MOST OF THE EARTH WAS COVERED WITH ICE, EARLY PEOPLE RELIED ON HUNTING FOR FOOD. THEY MAY HAVE PAINTED ANIMALS AS A KIND OF MAGIC TO ENSURE THERE WERE ALWAYS PLENTY.

OH NO! IT'S RAINING! QUICK! LET'S GET UNDER COVER.

HOW ABOUT THIS CAVE?

BRRR! IT'S FREEZING IN HERE!

CHEER UP! I'LL TRY TO MAKE A FIRE!

IT'S NOT VERY EASY! IF I WERE A CAVEMAN . . .

FRUSH

. . . I'D BE BETTER AT THIS!

ZZZZ . . . .

WELL DONE, MICKEY!

MICKEY?! WHERE ARE YOU? WHY DID YOU LEAVE ME AL . . . OOOH!

WOW! THIS IS AMAZING!

IT'S NOT REALLY THAT HARD TO DO.

YOU JUST NEED THE RIGHT COLORS! LOOK! I'VE MADE THEM BY MIXING EARTH AND WATER.

IT WAS JUST A DREAM.

IT'S NOT A DREAM. I'VE MADE AN AMAZING DISCOVERY!

AND THAT'S NOT ALL! COME AND SEE!

IT SEEMS THAT ONE OF YOUR ANCESTORS WAS A PREHISTORIC PAINTER.

OOH!

THAT'S QUITE POSSIBLE. IN FACT, NO MATTER HOW HARD I TRY...

...I ALWAYS DRAW EXACTLY LIKE A CAVEMAN!

HA! HA!

Chapter 2

Size

BEFORE THEY CAN begin a picture, artists have to decide what size to paint it. This may depend upon what the picture is for. Tiny pictures were made for one person to hold in the hand and gaze at closely in private. By contrast, kings asked artists to paint enormous portraits of themselves. These pictures were hung in their palaces to impress visitors and remind them of the king's power. Viewers could see them from afar and had to look up at them from below when they got close.

All puffed up

Important people asked artists to paint portraits of them as large as life. Since big pictures were costly and needed a large room to hang in, their size was a way of showing off a person's wealth. In the picture below, the sitters' haughty poses, the luxurious drapes, the pillars and the coat-of-arms all add to a feeling of grandeur.

Portrait of Govaert van Surpele(?) and his Wife 1636–8 **Jacob Jordaens**

**Portrait of Cornelis
van der Geest**
about 1620

Anthony van Dyck

Here's looking at you

Sometimes only a person's head
and shoulders are shown life-size,
as in this portrait. It feels as if
the man is very near you, looking
closely into a mirror, straight
into your eyes.

Room to swing a brush

An artist may need to use a large canvas because of *how* he paints. Jackson Pollock, an American artist, laid huge canvases on the floor, rather than on an easel. Using a stick or a hard, paint-caked brush, he swung his arm or flicked his wrist above the canvas, letting the paint drip, splash, splatter and swirl all over it. He moved around the entire canvas in a controlled, rhythmical way, almost dancing as he painted. The loops, swirls and curves of paint recorded the pattern of his movements.

ACTION PAINTING
Pollock's way of painting gave viewers a sense of his physical efforts in creating a picture. It was named "Action painting."

Number 3, 1949: Tiger 1949 **Jackson Pollock**

Pictures to fit a home

Many pictures, including these
two, were painted a convenient
size – neither too big nor too
small – to fit on the walls
of private homes. It is hard
to believe that these two are
almost the same size – about
the width and length of
a small kitchen tabletop.

Still Life with Oranges and Walnuts 1772 **Luis Meléndez**

**The Interior of
the Grote Kerk
at Haarlem**
1636–7

Pieter Saenredam

Detail

Large as life

Everything in Meléndez's picture *(left)* contains something good to eat, as large as life. You feel you could reach into the picture to crack one of the walnuts or pick up an orange.

What a B-I-G place

Saenredam's picture *(above)* is much the same size, but it makes you feel as if you could walk around an enormous church that stretches into the distance. The people dotted here and there give you an idea of how large the building is.

Small is beautiful

Small pictures draw in one viewer at a time, closer and closer. They are also easy to carry around.

Little is lovely

Over five hundred years ago, people hung small religious pictures in their homes to help them pray. One person at a time could kneel in front of this quiet picture and focus on every detail.

The Virgin and Child in an Interior about 1435

Workshop of Robert Campin (Jacques Daret?)

For my eyes only

Miniature portraits were made as loving keepsakes. People put them in lockets, worn secretly under clothes or openly as a piece of jewelry.

Prince Albert
William Charles Ross
1840

The Virgin and Child about 1485
Follower of Hugo van der Goes

Portable prayers

This tiny picture has a prayer written on the two hinged wings. These folded over the painting for protection when it was taken on a journey.

A tourist souvenir

Before photography and postcards were invented, Venetian artists earned a living by painting real and imaginary views of their famous city. Small postcard-size pictures, like this one, were perfect for visitors to take home as a reminder of their trip to Italy.

Caprice View with Ruins
after 1780

Francesco Guardi

Chapter 3

Shape

WHICH COMES FIRST, the shape of a picture or an artist's idea for an image? Sometimes artists make paintings to decorate existing objects, such as a fat, round vase, an oval plate or a rectangular chest. They fit the images they paint to the particular shape of the object. On the other hand, if artists start with an idea, they usually choose a shape that best suits it.

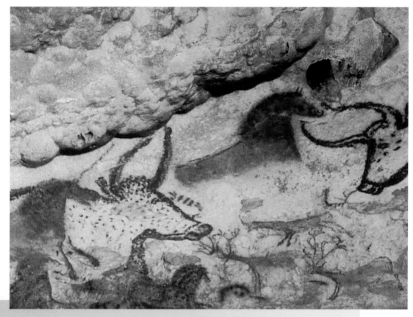

Cave paintings at Lascaux, France about 15,000 BC

Paintings on the walls

People made images long before they made
pictures on special surfaces with definite
shapes. Deep in dark, silent, hidden caves,
Old Stone Age people painted animals on
the rough, unprepared walls. They made
use of bumps to make an animal seem
rounded and solid. Sometimes, they
followed the curve of a smooth
ceiling to paint swiftly running bulls.

Painting within a shape

The ancient Greeks made jars for holding water, wine or oil. Artists painted the surface with characters and events from Greek myths or scenes of daily life, skillfully fitting the figures and animals around the curves.

Artists decorating everyday objects such as plates, furniture and kites, generally have to start with a fixed shape and fit different images within it.

Storage jar (amphora) showing Ajax and Achilles playing a game resembling backgammon

520 BC **Lysippides**

Venus and Mars
about 1485

Sandro Botticelli

Painted to fit

Rich parents sometimes gave their children
specially painted furniture as a wedding gift.
Botticelli probably painted this picture
on the footboard of a bed. It shows Venus,
goddess of Love, and Mars,
the god of War. Some impudent
baby fawns are trying
in vain to wake the
sleeping Mars. One
is blowing a conch shell
in his ear, while another
is wriggling under his arm.

Tall and thin

An artist who wanted to paint a portrait of one person from head to foot often chose a long, thin shape. This left no room for any distracting clutter on either side.

From top to toe

Centuries ago, kings married princesses from other countries without meeting them beforehand. Portraits were a way for them to see if they liked the look of their intended bride.

When King Henry VIII was looking for a fourth wife, he sent Holbein to paint a picture of this young woman (*right*). He trusted Holbein to show what she really looked like. Although Henry liked the picture, he did not marry Christina. Since he'd already had six wives – and had two of them beheaded – maybe Christina had a lucky escape!

Christina of Denmark,
Duchess of Milan
probably 1538

Hans Holbein the Younger

45

In the round

Your eye is usually attracted to the center of a circle. In this round picture, Mary and baby Jesus seem far away and yet they are the focus of attention, like the bull's-eye of a target. The crowd and the ruined buildings are painted along the lines of imaginary triangles that join at the center, pointing to Mary. Botticelli has left a gap in the foreground and a path through the center of the crowd for you to join in.

Detail

The Adoration of the Kings
about 1470–5
Sandro Botticelli

46

Odd shapes

Until the twentieth century,
most pictures were either
rectangular, round
or square.

Some modern artists
like to make odd-shaped
pictures, where the shape
itself is the subject of the picture.
Instead of leading your eye into
an imaginary space or place, the artist
tries to emphasize how flat a picture is.

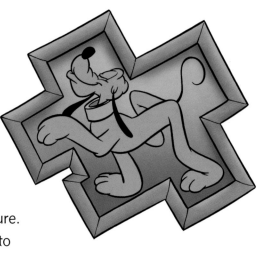

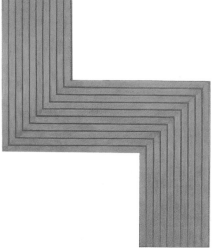

Stella's stripes

In Stella's picture *(left)*, the
stripes exactly follow the shape
of the canvas. They have been
carefully measured, so they are
all the same distance apart.

Ophir
1960–1
Frank Stella

What do you remember?

Choose the best answer to finish each sentence.
Look back at chapters 2 and 3 to help you.

1

Miniature portraits were painted for people's:
a) wallets
b) lockets
c) pockets

4

Old Stone Age people painted images of:
a) fighting dinosaurs
b) running bulls
c) apples and pears

2

The Ancient Greeks gave painted pots to the winners of:
a) gardening competitions
b) painting and sculpture competitions
c) athletic and music competitions

3

Venetian artists painted views of their city:
a) to sell to tourists
b) to hang in local cafés
c) to illustrate magazines

5

Jackson Pollock's way of painting is known as:
a) acrobatic painting
b) active painting
c) action painting

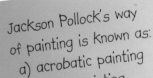

Holbein painted a full-length portrait of Christina:

a) to show off her fine clothes
b) to show whether she looked pretty and healthy
c) as a birthday present for King Henry VIII of England

Meléndez's picture of food (on page 36) includes:
a) grapes and lemons
b) apples and dates
c) oranges and a melon

7

Large portraits displayed a person's:
a) wealth
b) greediness
c) shyness

10

People hung small religious pictures at home:
a) to show off
b) to help them pray
c) so they would not have to go to church

8

Venus is the goddess of:
a) flowers and vegetables
b) love and beauty
c) food and wine

Answers

1b, 2c, 3a, 4b, 5c, 6b, 7a, 8b, 9c, 10b

49

MICKEY BUYS A DUTCH PICTURE

MICKEY AND MINNIE ARE ADMIRING A WINTRY LANDSCAPE IN THE NATIONAL GALLERY, IN LONDON. IT WAS PAINTED BY AVERCAMP, WHO LIVED IN HOLLAND BETWEEN 1585 AND 1634. DUTCH ARTISTS IN THE 1600s CELEBRATED THEIR COUNTRY BY PAINTING PICTURES FOR WEALTHY PEOPLE TO BUY FOR THEIR HOMES.

WHAT A LIVELY PICTURE!

DID YOU KNOW ONE OF MY ANCESTORS HAD A HAND IN IT?

MICHAEL VAN DER MOUSE WAS A DUTCH ARCHITECT WHO HAD SOME VERY DIFFICULT CLIENTS.

UM...YES! EXCEPT FOR THE FAR WALL, WHICH LOOKS RATHER BARE.

MASTER MICHAEL, YOU'VE DONE AN EXCELLENT JOB.

THAT'S WAITING FOR A PAINTING. I WANT YOU TO CHOOSE ONE. FOLLOW ME!

OH, I DO LOVE TO SEE PEOPLE SKATING!

ME TOO! IF ONLY IT WASN'T SO...

... COLD! BRRR! LET'S HURRY UP!

HOW ABOUT THIS ONE?

IT'S GREAT!

I DON'T LIKE IT! IT MAKES ME FEEL SEASICK.

MUCH BETTER TO STAY ON DRY LAND!

DRY? WITH ALL THAT MUD?

I THINK THIS ONE WOULD BE PERFECT FOR OUR DINING ROOM.

AREN'T YOU FORGETTING THAT I AM ALLERGIC TO LOBSTER?

I DON'T WANT COWS IN OUR HOUSE. THEY ATTRACT FLIES!

AND FLOWERS ATTRACT BEES.

WHY DON'T YOU COMMISSION THE GREAT REMBRANDT TO DO A PORTRAIT OF YOU BOTH?

OOH, THAT'S A WONDERFUL IDEA!

NO IT ISN'T. I COULDN'T BEAR . . .

. . . STANDING STILL LIKE THIS FOR HOURS ON END.

ISN'T THERE ANYTHING THEY MIGHT BOTH LIKE?

MMM. LET ME THINK.

WHY DO YOU ALWAYS DISAGREE?

ME? IT'S YOU THAT NEVER AGREES.

I'VE GOT AN IDEA. IS THERE A PAINTER WHO COULD. . . ?

BZZZ

BZZZ

OF COURSE! DUTCH PAINTERS CAN DO ANYTHING!

WELL, THE PROBLEM OF THE BARE WALL IS SOLVED.

I DON'T SEE HOW. WE HAVEN'T CHOSEN ANYTHING YET.

WAIT AND SEE!

A FEW DAYS LATER...

A ROUND WINDOW! AND WHAT A BEAUTIFUL VIEW!

MASTER MICHAEL, WHAT A GREAT IDEA!

BUT HANG ON... *THAT* ISN'T THE VIEW FROM HERE!

?

AS A MATTER OF FACT, THIS ISN'T A REAL WINDOW...

...THE VIEW IS YOUR NEW PAINTING. NOW YOU'LL BE ABLE...

...TO LOOK AT A SCENE THAT YOU *BOTH* LIKE AND WITHOUT GETTING COLD!

THAT WAS VERY CLEVER OF YOUR ANCESTOR!

WELL... I CERTAINLY TAKE AFTER SOMEONE, DON'T I?

Chapter 4

Color

ARTISTS USE COLOR to make pictures sing.
If they want to make things look lusciously
lifelike, they use colors that match the colors
of the real things. But colors can also communicate
feelings, temperature or ideas. Colors can make
a picture feel cheerful and full of energy, cosy and
quiet or cold and dismal. An artist's choice of
color may tickle our senses or stir our emotions,
to please, surprise or upset us.

McLEAN COUNTY UNIT #5
105-CARLOCK

Fruit and
Flowers in a
Terracotta Vase
1777–78

Jan van Os

True colors . . .

Some artists were highly skilled at painting
things to look extremely true to life. Van Os
was famous for his realistic still life paintings
(*above*). He carefully shaded the colors of
each fruit and flower to show its particular texture.

Detail

. . . but not true to life

But the arrangement is not true
to life at all. Tulips flower in
spring, roses bloom in summer,
grapes ripen in the autumn, and
a pineapple is far too heavy to
balance on the top. Van Os
took a year to do this picture,
painting each fruit and flower
as it came into season. So
although the artist had seen
real plums, rose hips, birds'
nests and everything else he
painted, this display could never
have existed outside a picture.

Wealth and beauty

This picture *(below)* of a rich banker's wife has been painted to show off her wealth, as well as her beauty. Look how precisely the artist has painted the colors and details of her jewelry, chintz dress and grand furnishings.

Madame Moitessier
1856

Jean-Auguste-Dominique Ingres

Details

The Water-Lily Pond 1899 **Claude-Oscar Monet**

Detail

Mingling colors

Monet was intrigued by how light fell on the lily pond in his garden and changed its color from one moment to the next. Here he painted exactly the colors he saw when the pond was bathed in dancing sunlight. But he didn't paint every leaf or petal in detail. Instead, he built up layers of different greens and blues to give an impression of the plants, water and the shadows, adding dabs of pink and crimson for the water lilies. Hold up the book and squint at the picture to see the glinting effect of light.

**Right-hand panel
of The Wilton Diptych**
about 1395–9

**English or French,
unknown artist**

Heavenly blue

No one has ever seen heaven, yet hundreds of years ago, people imagined that it must be blue and gold – the colors of the sky and the sun.

The painter of this picture used real gold leaf and a precious blue, made of crushed lapis lazuli, for the robes of the Virgin Mary and her angels in heaven.

Combing the Hair about 1896   **Hilaire-Germain-Edgar Degas**

Red hot and cool blue

Colors can suggest different moods and temperatures. The sky and sea are often blue, so blue is seen as cool and fresh. Fiery reds and oranges suggest heat and energy. Blood-red can mean danger and pain. Some artists have used the power of individual colors to express a particular atmosphere in their pictures. Degas used all sorts of reds in this picture to suggest the heat of the room and the discomfort of the woman having her long hair brushed.

Sunflowers 1888 **Vincent van Gogh**

Sunny yellow

Van Gogh used colors to create a mood in his paintings. He thought that yellow, his favorite color, could make everyone feel happy and hopeful. He painted this very yellow picture when he was looking forward to the visit of Gauguin, another artist. He hung it in his friend's room to welcome him.

Boating on the Seine about 1879–80 **Pierre-Auguste Renoir**

Dazzling reflections

Artists have always known that some colors look brighter together than on their own. See how the blues and oranges in the picture above create the effect of the dazzle of a hot summer's day on the river. Side by side, the blues seem bluer and the oranges more orange, and both seem to shimmer.

Detail

Complementary colors

By the nineteenth century, people could explain scientifically why this happens.

On this color wheel (*right*), primary colors (red, blue and yellow) and secondary colors (green, orange and purple) which are made from two primaries, are opposite each other. These pairs – red and green; blue and orange; yellow and purple – are known as complementary colors.

Glowing colours

Placed next to one another, complementary colors look stronger and more intense. So next to orange or purple, red looks dull. But next to green, its complementary color, red stands out much more and both colors appear to flicker.

Red alert

Was your eye caught by this little boy drinking from a stream in the picture below? The artist deliberately painted his vest red to make him stand out from the greenery. This splash of bright color also makes the boy seem nearer to you than the trees and the golden fields.

Detail

The Cornfield
1826

John Constable

Christ teaching from Saint Peter's Boat on the Lake of Gennesaret 1667
Herman Saftleven

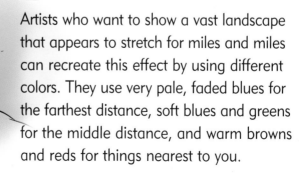

The blue hills far away

When you are outside and can see into the far distance, things farthest from you appear to fade into a pale blue haze.

Artists who want to show a vast landscape that appears to stretch for miles and miles can recreate this effect by using different colors. They use very pale, faded blues for the farthest distance, soft blues and greens for the middle distance, and warm browns and reds for things nearest to you.

Chapter 5

Light and Dark

A S WELL AS using color to create a mood or temperature, artists also rely on light and dark. Just like a spotlight in a theater, light can pick out important details in a picture. Dark shadows can create an atmosphere of mystery and strangeness. Artists use white for the lightest highlights and black for the darkest shadows, but can also create contrasts with colors.

The Nativity, at Night late 15th century **Geertgen tot Sint Jans**

See how your eyes are drawn to each of the three brightly lit parts of this picture.

They shine out of the darkness, to highlight different events in the Christmas story.

The highlights

The glowing baby Jesus sends out glittering beams, lighting up the amazed faces of Mary and the angels surrounding the crib.

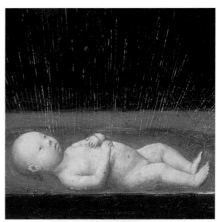

Another angel shines in the sky, announcing the news to the shepherds huddled around their flickering fire on the hillside.

Find the shadowy figure of Joseph and a cow and a donkey in the darkness of the stable.

LIGHT AND DARK

Peasants under the Trees at Dawn   about 1840–5   **Jean-Baptiste-Camille Corot**

Early risers

What time is it in the picture above?
The colors and shadows give
you a clue.

The long, pale shadows fall
toward you and the pearly light
in the sky comes from behind the
dark houses. This is how things
would look just after sunrise.

A night out in Paris

In this picture, the warm, bright glow of the streetlamps and lighted shops contrasts strongly with the color of the sky to suggest a nighttime scene.

The artist has painted smudgy dabs to show people bustling along the street and broken brushstrokes to conjure up glistening reflections of the lights on the wet road and sidewalks.

The Boulevard Montmartre at Night 1897 **Camille Pissarro**

Lurking in the shadows

Bold contrasts of light and dark
can also make a scene seem very
mysterious. In this picture, the bright
shaft of sunlight streaming through
the big windows lights up only the back wall
of the room. The rest is so dark that it's hard
to make out what the man looks like, what
he is doing or what is on the barely visible shelves.

*A Man seated
reading at a Table
in a Lofty Room*
about 1631–50

**Follower of
Rembrandt**

Noon at night

Artists can play tricks with light and show things which would be impossible to see in real life. Magritte wanted to make people think twice about his work. He painted this scene to look as realistic as possible. But it could never be daytime in the sky and nighttime on earth at the same time, like this.

Empire of Lights 1949 **René Magritte**

Still Life with a Pewter Flagon and Two Ming Bowls
1649 **Jan Jansz. Treck**

White and gray

If you could touch the objects in the picture above, which ones would feel polished or rough, squashy or knobbly? Using light and shade, as well as color, artists can make you sense how things feel and what they are made of.

Gray shadows crumple the soft, white cloth. White patches on the flagon show how reflective its shiny surface is.

Notice from the reflections and shadows how the light is shining from the left.

Colored shadows

Using color, bright yellow and darkest blue, Matisse shows you how hot and bright it is outside his window and how much darker and cooler it is indoors.

Landscape viewed from a Window
1912

Henri Matisse

How sharp are your eyes?

Choose the best answer to these questions.
Use chapters 4 and 5 to help you.

1

Where is this man sitting?
a) in a room
b) on a street corner
c) outside a café

4

Where is this streetlamp?
a) outside a house
b) on a seaside pier
c) in the middle of a street

2

Who is pulling on this oar?
a) a girl with short blonde hair
b) a boy with a white cap
c) a girl with long dark hair

5

Is this a detail of:
a) a flower?
b) a skirt?
c) a curtain?

3

Where is this glowing fire?
a) in an open fireplace
b) on a hillside
c) in a forest

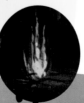

6

What time of day does this show?
a) dawn
b) midday
c) dusk

7

Where are these people?
a) on a beach
b) in a cornfield
c) in a garden

10

Who painted this sunflower?
a) Monet
b) Renoir
c) Van Gogh

8

Where can you find these flowers?
a) growing in a garden
b) arranged in a vase
c) in a bouquet that someone is holding

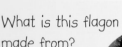

11

What is this flagon made from?
a) silver
b) pewter
c) leather

9

Is this angel looking at:
a) the Virgin Mary?
b) baby Jesus?
c) another angel?

12

Where are these boats?
a) on a lake
b) out at sea
c) on a river

77

MICKEY HELPS AN IMPRESSIONIST

MICKEY AND MINNIE ARE IN THE NATIONAL GALLERY, LONDON, LOOKING AT A VIEW OF STEAM ENGINES IN THE PARIS RAILWAY STATION OF ST. LAZARE.
IT WAS PAINTED IN 1877 BY MONET. HE PAINTED TWELVE DIFFERENT VIEWS OF THIS STATION.

DID YOU KNOW ONE OF MY ANCESTORS HELPED MONET TO PAINT THIS?

WAS HE A PAINTER TOO?

NO! AN ENGINEER.

ONE DAY MICHEL WAS WITH HIS NEPHEWS IN HIS LOCOMOTIVE

UNCLE MICHEL! LOOK . . .

WHAT A FUNNY BOAT!

THAT'S THE STUDIO OF MY FRIEND MONET, THE PAINTER. WOULD YOU LIKE TO VISIT IT?

OH, YES

AND SO . . .

WELCOME ABOARD, MY FRIENDS, BUT FORGIVE ME A MOMENT . . .

... WHILE I PUT THE FINAL TOUCHES TO MY PAINTING!

THERE! ALL FINISHED!

IT DOESN'T LOOK VERY FINISHED TO ME.

NO, BUT I REALLY LIKE IT.

I'M TRYING TO CATCH THE SHIFTING SUNLIGHT, SO I HAVE TO PAINT VERY FAST.

YOU CERTAINLY MANAGE TO PAINT A LOT OF PICTURES!

BUT ONLY IN SUNNY WEATHER. IN WINTER, I'LL BE IN BIG TROUBLE!

OH! WHY?

BECAUSE I WON'T BE ABLE TO WORK OUTDOORS. THE DAYS ARE SHORT, THE LIGHT'S DULL AND IT'LL BE FREEZING COLD...

... AND EVEN IF I COULD, WHO'D BUY BLEAK WINTRY VIEWS OF THE RIVER?

IF I CAN'T FIND SOMEWHERE ELSE TO PAINT, HOW WILL I BE ABLE TO SUPPORT MY FAMILY?

UHM . . .

I'VE GOT IT! I KNOW A PLACE WHERE YOU CAN WORK OUTDOORS WITHOUT WORRYING ABOUT RAIN OR SNOW . . .

. . . AND PEOPLE WILL REALLY WANT TO BUY WHAT YOU PAINT. TRUST ME!

A FEW MONTHS LATER . . .

THIS IS WONDERFUL. I'M UNDER COVER, WARMED BY THE STEAM OF THE ENGINES, AND . . .

80

... THANKS TO THE GLASS ROOF, IT'S JUST AS IF I WERE OUTDOORS! I CAN PAINT VIEWS BOTH INSIDE AND OUTSIDE THE STATION.

AND YOU WERE RIGHT! PEOPLE LIKE THESE PICTURES OF MODERN LIFE. THERE'S JUST ONE PROBLEM ...

I'D LIKE TO SHOW THE STATION WITH CLOUDS OF STEAM, BUT THE TRAINS LEAVE TOO QUICKLY!

IS THAT ALL?

AND SO ...

THIS ENGINE HAS BEEN CHUFFING FOR OVER AN HOUR! WHEN IS THE TRAIN LEAVING?

DON'T ASK ME ...

... ASK MONSIEUR MONET!

NICE STORY!

YES! MICHEL LOST HIS JOB BECAUSE HIS TRAINS RAN LATE – BUT WHAT A MASTERPIECE HE HELPED PRODUCE!

81

Chapter 6

Where are You?

PICTURES ARE AS flat as pancakes and small enough to fit on a wall. But artists have discovered ways of creating a feeling of space and distance in their paintings. They can take you on imaginary journeys to faraway places. They make you believe that you can see views that stretch away into the distance. They can even trick your eyes into thinking you are actually inside a picture.

What a view!

Artists may invite you to stand beside them and gaze at their painted view from one chosen viewpoint. They can make you believe you are high up or low down by where they put the horizon line – where the land meets the sky.

A picture with a high horizon line, like the one below, creates the distinct illusion that you are standing on a high mountaintop, looking down at the rocky valleys and the far distant peaks.

A picture with a low horizon line, like the one on the right, encourages you to step on to an uncrowded, windy beach and watch the clouds float by.

The Valley of St-Vincent probably 1830   **Pierre-Etienne-Théodore Rousseau**

A normal viewpoint

A high viewpoint

A low viewpoint

Hold the book at arm's length, with the dotted line level with your eyes. Compare the difference between the horizon lines.

Putting you in the picture

If you stand in the middle of a straight road, you will notice that in the distance, the sides of the road seem to meet at a point known as the vanishing point, on the horizon. Hobbema used the same visual effect to pull us inside his picture (*below*). We are made to believe we are walking down the middle of the muddy road, to greet the man coming toward us.

Detail

The Avenue at Middelharnis
1689

Meindert Hobbema

As far as the eye can see

Hobbema planned his painting very precisely to give an impression of great distance. The treetops seem to lead downward and the sides of the road seem to lead upward. They all meet at the vanishing point, which appears to be a long way away.

Meeting on the road

Hobbema deliberately placed the head of the man exactly on the vanishing point. Our gaze is drawn straight down the long tree-lined road toward him. He looks back at us, his eyes level with ours.

Seeing into the distance

In real life, faraway things look smaller than they really are. Hobbema has painted the trees gradually smaller to create the same effect in his picture.

Near and far

The spindly tree trunks overlap the land and buildings beyond. This makes you feel that the trees are in front of them.

Fading into the distance

Another way artists can suggest a feeling of distance is by painting the people and buildings farthest away paler and fuzzier than those in the foreground. Compare the size and the detail of these figures below, shown in scale from the picture above.

The Market Place and the Grote Kerk at Haarlem
1674

Gerrit Berckheyde

Details

Under the arches

This picture makes you feel as if you are sheltering in the shade of an arcade, looking out at a sunny square in Venice. Think how high the tower must be if it looks this tall from a distance.

Venice: Piazza San Marco
about 1756
Canaletto

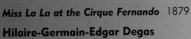

Miss La La at the Cirque Fernando 1879

Hilaire-Germain-Edgar Degas

Looking up . . .

Do you want to crane your head to look up at Miss La La (*left*) dangling by her teeth? The artist has tried to capture the experience of being at the circus, watching this daring performance with bated breath. Miss La La is painted from the viewpoint of the audience below, to make you feel that you are taking part as well. The clashing oranges and greens add to the excitement.

. . . and down

The angle of this sturdy, rush-seated chair invites you to sit down – at least, once you've removed the pipe and tobacco! The chair belonged to the artist. He painted it to show how he was inspired by everyday, natural things.

Van Gogh's Chair
1888
Vincent van Gogh

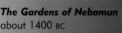

The Gardens of Nebamun
about 1400 BC

From a tomb in Thebes

Which way is up?

Ancient Egyptian artists painted things from whatever viewpoint made them the most recognizable, rather than as they saw them in real life.

This tomb painting fragment *(above)* is typical of a picture done from several viewpoints.

The pond is seen from above, to display its exact shape. But the fish, ducks and floating flowers are pictured from the side, since this is how they are easiest to identify. The plants and trees around the pool are painted sideways, to show that they form a border all around it.

Climb every mountain

Chinese painters tried to create views that lead your eye on a journey, usually to a far distant mountain. The journey begins on a path at the bottom of a painting. The path zigzags up the picture to the top of the mountain. The tall, narrow-shaped picture emphasizes the height of the mountain.

Air and clouds are shown as empty spaces in between the solid objects, such as rocks, mountains and trees. These create a feeling of distance and time passing on the journey.

The Emperor Kuang-wu fording a river
16th century

Ch'iu Ying

Being there

A very close viewpoint can make you feel you are part of a picture. In the scene below, the artist places you in this candlelit room with the musicians.

The flute player and the woman glance over their shoulders toward you, to see who is disturbing their concert. You are made to feel so close, you could touch the grapes.

The Concert about 1626 **Hendrick ter Brugghen**

I and the Village 1911 **Marc Chagall**

Distant memories

Sometimes artists create a sense of distance to suggest the past, as well as to show somewhere faraway. This artist painted a big image of his face as a grown-up. Behind him are the small wooden houses he remembered from his childhood village. The artist painted them very small, and some even upside-down, to show they are a jumble of memories and dreams about his homeland.

Chapter 7

A hole in the Wall

SOMETIMES ARTISTS INCLUDE a realistic-looking window frame, arch or step as part of their painting. These separate us from the world the artist has created inside the picture. People and objects appear to be inside their own space or to come out into ours.

Step right in

The stone step in Crivelli's picture *(right)* separates our world from his ideal, imaginary one. Notice how the cucumber seems to balance on the step – as if half-in and half-out of the picture.

Details

Our gaze is led straight down the street – past the decorated buildings and through the arch to the window in the wall at the far end.

The Annunciation, with Saint Emidius 1486 **Carlo Crivelli**

Saint Jerome in his Study about 1475

Antonello da Messina

Take a peek

A realistic stone arch with a window ledge frames the view of Saint Jerome's study (*left*). This makes it seem as if you were taking a peek into the room from outside. You can see right across the room to another view beyond. Watch out for the saint's pet lion standing in the shadows.

Details

Portrait of a Woman (Marie Larp?)
about 1635–8
Frans Hals

Sitting pretty

Is this woman sitting behind an oval window or inside a picture frame? The shadows in the picture give you a clue. The shadows on the frame make you think it is solid, as if you were looking through a real opening. The shadow behind the woman makes you feel that she is sitting in a room looking out at you.

Look twice

Can you see the clever trick this artist has played (*right*)? He painted a half-length likeness of himself within a frame. But his hand comes outside it. So, in fact, he has painted himself as a person *behind* the frame, not as a picture *inside* it. But the frame is on a shelf with a wall behind, so where is the rest of his body?

Self Portrait
probably 1670–3
Bartolomé Esteban Murillo

The little girl (*below right*) has been painted *inside* the picture, but *outside* the frame.

A Little Girl
about 1520
Jan Gossaert

What's the answer?

Choose the best answer to finish these 10 sentences.
Look back at chapters 6 and 7 to help you.

1

This little girl is wearing:
a) a blue silk tunic
b) a red velvet bodice
c) a purple cotton apron

3

In Chinese pictures, clouds are shown as:
a) white blobs
b) empty spaces
c) thick streaks

4

Saint Jerome's pet was:
a) a lamb
b) a cheetah
c) a lion

2

The point where the land meets the sky is called:
a) the horizon
b) the viewpoint
c) the vanishing point

5

This performer was called:
a) Miss Fa Fa
b) Miss Ra Ra
c) Miss La La

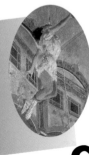

6

This woman's right hand is:
a) on her lap
b) held to her chest
c) out of sight

9

This child is peeping on to:
a) a square in Venice
b) a market scene
c) a street

7

This picture has been painted from:
a) a high viewpoint
b) a low viewpoint
c) a normal viewpoint

10

To make things look far away, artists paint them:
a) darker
b) fuzzier
c) bigger

8

This artist has painted himself as:
a) a picture in a frame
b) a person outside a frame
c) a person behind a frame

Answers

MICKEY AND THE SECRET OF THE MONA LISA'S SMILE

MICKEY AND MINNIE ARE AT THE LOUVRE MUSEUM IN PARIS. THEY STOP IN FRONT OF LEONARDO DA VINCI'S PORTRAIT OF MONA LISA, PAINTED AROUND 1505, FAMOUS FOR ITS MYSTERIOUS SMILE. LEONARDO, A GREAT ITALIAN ARTIST, WAS BORN IN 1452. HE DIED IN FRANCE IN 1519. HE SPENT YEARS DESIGNING, WITHOUT SUCCESS, A MACHINE THAT WOULD ENABLE PEOPLE TO FLY LIKE BIRDS.

HAVE YOU HEARD THE STORY ABOUT HOW OUR ANCESTORS HELPED LEONARDO PAINT THIS FAMOUS PICTURE?

MY ANCESTOR, MICHELETTO, WAS A PIGMENT SELLER. ONE DAY, HE WENT TO LEONARDO'S HOUSE...

WELCOME, MY LAD. SHOW ME WHAT YOU'VE GOT!

HAVE YOU GOT ANY DRAGONSBLOOD FOR MAKING RED GLAZE?

SORRY! I DON'T HAVE ANY.

NEVER MIND. WOULD YOU LIKE TO SEE MY STUDIO?

I'D LOVE TO!

MONA MINNA, WHY DON'T YOU SHOW THIS YOUNG MAN OUR LATEST MASTERPIECE?

LATEST? WE'VE BEEN WORKING ON IT FOR THREE YEARS!

106

WELL, WE CAN'T DO ANY MORE TODAY. MONA LISA'S GONE HOME.

IT'S A PITY SHE LOOKS SO GRUMPY.

MAYBE YOU COULD PAINT HER A SMILE, WHILE I TALK TO THIS YOUNG MAN?

I'D BE HONORED TO TRY, MASTER.

BLAH, BLAH . . . AND WHEN I'VE WORKED OUT HOW TO FLY, I THOUGHT I'D INVENT . . .

YOU SEEM MORE INTERESTED IN MONA MINNA THAN IN LISTENING TO ME.

HUH?

SO YOU WERE SAYING . . .

YIKES!

107

Chapter 8

Speedy and Still

WHEN YOU STAND still, sit at a table or lie down, your body is restful, steady and balanced. It is either vertical (upright) or horizontal (going from side to side).

As soon as you walk,
run or jump, your body leans
off balance in one direction or another.

Similarly, artists paint lines and shapes
at different angles to make you believe that
their pictures are either still or full of movement.

Dutch Ships in a Calm
about 1660

Willem van de Velde the Younger

Small Dutch Vessels in a Breeze
after 1660

Studio of Willem van de Velde

Calm *before* the storm

To show there is no wind *(top left* and *right)*, the artist has painted ships lying flat in the water, with their masts and sails upright. Even some of the sailors are standing up to work. The clear reflections in the glassy sea echo these horizontal and vertical shapes.

Details

Storm at sea

To suggest the force of windy weather *(bottom left* and *above)*, the artist has painted the boats and sailors leaning at an angle.

The choppy waves lead your eyes and drive the boats toward the edge of the picture, out into the unseen sea beyond.

Rain, Steam and Speed – The Great Western Railway before 1844
Joseph Mallord William Turner

Watch out for the train

Trains had only recently been invented when this picture was painted. The artist tried to capture the excitement that people must have felt at traveling faster than they ever had before. Imagine sighting one of these steaming black monsters coming toward you. The artist makes you believe you are standing by the bridge, about to see this train hurtle past. Thick swirls and slashes of paint suggest heavy, driving rain, which break up the shape of the speeding train.

In the eye of the storm

Rousseau has painted his stormy scene in crisp detail. The leaves, branches and blades of grass bend over in the strong wind. Slanting streaks of rain lash across the jungle. Flashes of lightning snake through the sky. The tiger crouches in the grass, his eyes wide. He is either about to pounce on some unseen prey or is hiding in fear of the storm.

Detail

Tiger in a Tropical Storm (Surprised!)
1891

Henri Rousseau

What's the big hurry?

Early in the twentieth century, a new photographic technique was invented. It could show a sequence of actions, frozen one on top of another, in the same photo. This inspired several artists to try painting movement in a similar way.

In this funny picture *(below)*, the overlapping blurred images of a woman's feet and her dog give a lively impression of them scurrying along at top speed.

Dynamism of a Dog on a Leash
1912
Giacomo Balla

116

A moving experience

Hold the book up with this picture at eye
level and stare hard at it. Does it seem
to move? Can you see how the painter
has altered some of the squares of this black-
and-white checkerboard pattern? This fools
your brain into thinking that some parts of
the picture are throbbing or flickering.

Supernovae
1959 – 1961

Victor Vasarely

A Young Woman standing at a Virginal
about 1670

Jan Vermeer

As still as a statue

The woman stands in the middle of this painting,
as still and erect as a statue. She stares out
of the picture with a shy smile. Perhaps she
is waiting for you to sit down on the empty
chair to join her in a song. The pale light
and the cool blues and creams make
the scene feel very calm and private.

The Baptism of Christ
1450s

Piero della Francesca

Total peace

To create this calm and balanced picture, the artist used geometry to work out the position of everything. See how the painting is made up of an overlapping square and circle. Christ stands perfectly still in the very center of the square and the Holy Dove hovers above him in the center of the circle. The mirror-like water reflects the hills behind him.

Chapter 9

Noisy and Quiet

Pictures can't make any sound, so how can artists make you believe that their paintings are noisy or quiet?

Just as people can shout loudly or murmur softly, artists can use noisy, bright colors or quiet, muted ones.

Just as you can hear sharp, piercing screams or a gentle sigh, artists can use spiky, jagged shapes or soothing round ones to hint at different sounds.

Bacchus and Ariadne 1522–3 **Titian**

What a commotion!

It's no wonder that Ariadne, the woman
in blue and red, stops and turns around in
alarm to see what all the noise is. Bacchus,
the god of wine, is leaping off his chariot to
propose to her. His noisy friends follow behind
and a barking dog adds to the hullabaloo.

Detail

Who's making all that noise?

The picture is full of sound and fury. Colors clamor, a tambourine rattles and cymbals clash. Stamping their feet, the people whoop and yell. Titian has painted each person twisting in action, with an arm raised or a knee bent.

The bright blue triangle of sea and sky set against the earth colors adds to the feeling of energy. The only still creatures are the two cheetahs, who gaze quietly at each other.

Details

Details

Can you hear the sirens?

The gleaming gold and sizzling red summon up the deafening noise and speed of a firetruck zooming down a dark street. The numbers change size as the truck rushes along, at top speed, with its sirens wailing.

I Saw the Figure 5 in Gold 1928 **Charles Demuth**

Colonel Banastre Tarleton
1782
Sir Joshua Reynolds

The noise of battle

This picture celebrates an English soldier who fought in America's Revolutionary War. Proud in his crisp, clean uniform, he posed for this portrait in the painter's studio – hands at the ready on his sword and one foot raised. In the background, the painter imagined the noisy chaos of war. Banging cannons smoke and flames crackle. Horses whinny and rear in alarm at the din.

Quietly on his own

Ssh! Don't disturb this quiet boy.
One hasty move and his house
of cards will fall down. The artist
created a calm mood by painting
the boy in a restful, upright pose,
with his arm flat on the table.
He also used warm, soft, muted
colors. The harmony between
the colors of his jacket and the
plain walls hushes the atmosphere.

The House of Cards about 1736–7 **Jean-Siméon Chardin**

Winter Landscape
probably 1811

Caspar David Friedrich

Detail

A silent prayer

Nothing seems to stir in this hushed landscape, muffled in snow. The ghostly silhouette of a church looms out of the mist, echoing the shape of the still fir trees. But look closer.

A lame man leans against a rock, his hands joined in prayer. The huge trees make him seem tiny and alone. But he has thrown away his crutches and the sky is turning pink with the coming of dawn, so maybe his silent prayers will be answered.

True or False?

Are these statements true or false?
Look back at chapters 8 and 9 to help you find the answers.

1 There is a tiger hiding in this jungle.

This boy is playing dominoes.

2 Bacchus is the god of wind.

3 This train is speeding over a bridge.

This woman is washing up.

5

6

This way of painting movement was inspired by photography.

9

A falcon is hovering over Jesus' head.

7

This soldier was an American hero.

10

Diagonal lines create a sense of movement.

8

This man is rubbing his hands to keep warm in the snow.

MICKEY AND TITIAN'S NOISY PICTURE

MICKEY AND MINNIE ARE ENJOYING A FAMOUS PICTURE AT THE NATIONAL GALLERY PAINTED BY THE GREAT VENETIAN ARTIST, TITIAN. HE WAS BORN SOMETIME BETWEEN 1470 AND 1480 AND DIED IN 1576. THE PAINTING SHOWS A MOMENT FROM A GREEK MYTH, WHEN BACCHUS, THE GOD OF WINE, FALLS IN LOVE WITH A PRINCESS CALLED ARIADNE.

NOISY?

THIS PAINTING IS WONDERFUL. IT'S SO . . . SO . . .

YES! THAT'S THE RIGHT WORD. BUT HOW DO YOU . . .

ONE OF MY ANCESTORS WAS TITIAN'S ERRAND BOY . . .

MASTER TITIAN! AN ENVOY FROM THE DUKE OF FERRARA IS ASKING TO SEE YOU.

OH, NO! HE'LL WANT TO KNOW HOW THE DUKE'S PICTURE IS PROGRESSING!

. . . AND HE HELPED THE ARTIST GET THIS PICTURE FINISHED ON TIME.

QUITE RIGHT, MASTER TITIAN! BUT AS FAR AS I CAN SEE . . .

. . . YOU ARE A LONG WAY FROM FINISHING IT!

THE THING IS . . . I PAINT IN OILS AND THEY TAKE A LONG TIME TO DRY.

THAT'S AS MAY BE. BUT THE DUKE IS IMPATIENT, SO I'LL HAVE TO MAKE SURE THAT YOUR WORK SPEEDS UP . . .

I SHALL COME BACK AND SEE YOU SOON. VERY SOON!

OOF!

THE MASTER'S VERY UPSET. HE JUST WANTS TO BE LEFT TO WORK IN PEACE AND QUIET.

MAYBE IF HE HAD TO GO AND WORK AT THE DUKE'S CASTLE IN FERRARA, HE WOULD PAINT MORE QUICKLY.

BUT SINCE HE PAINTS ON CANVAS, HE HAS NO NEED TO LEAVE HOME, BECAUSE EVEN HIS BIGGEST PICTURES CAN BE ROLLED UP AND SENT ANYWHERE.

AND AT HOME, HE CAN WORK ON SEVERAL PICTURES AT ONCE, SO THEY'RE ALL LATE!

EVEN WORSE, WHEN THE MODELS GET BORED AND GO AWAY, IT'S UP TO ME TO FIND NEW ONES.

MAYBE THE ENVOY'S VISITS WILL MAKE HIM SPEED UP.

TSK! IT WOULD TAKE MORE THAT A DUKE'S ENVOY TO DISTURB THE PEACE AND QUIET OF THIS STUDIO. ON THE OTHER HAND . . .

.. MAYBE WITH A LITTLE HELP ...

?

A LITTLE LATER ...

WHAT'S THE MEANING OF THIS HORRIBLE RACKET? WHO ARE ALL THESE PEOPLE?

THE NEW MODELS, MASTER! I COULDN'T FIND ANY PROFESSIONALS, SO I HAD TO MAKE DO WITH THIS BUNCH!

HURRY UP, MASTER! I HAVE TO GET DINNER READY!

HEY, YOU WON'T COOK MY EELS, WILL YOU?

EELS?

WELL ... I COULDN'T FIND THE SNAKES YOU WANTED.

YAP! YAP! YAP!

AND YOU! WHAT ARE YOU YAPPING FOR?

HE'S JEALOUS. WHY NOT PUT HIM IN THE PICTURE? THEN HE MIGHT CALM DOWN.

I'LL DO JUST THAT... AND AS FAST AS POSSIBLE. I CAN'T WAIT TO GET RID OF THIS NOISY LOT!

HEE, HEE! YES! AND THE NOISIER THEY ARE, THE SOONER THE MASTER WILL FINISH HIS PICTURE!

YOU CHOSE THOSE ROWDY PEOPLE ON PURPOSE!

WILL YOU PLEASE KEEP STILL... AND QUIET AS WELL?!!

EXCUSE ME! THE DUKE WANTS THESE CHEETAHS, THE PRIDE OF HIS MENAGERIE, INCLUDED IN THE PICTURE.

TELL THE DUKE THAT'S FINE...

...AND THAT THE PICTURE WILL BE PAINTED EVEN SOONER IF HE SENDS OVER THE LIVE MODELS! TEE-HEE!

?

SO DID HE PAINT THIS PICTURE REALLY QUICKLY?

I DON'T KNOW. BUT CERTAINLY NO OTHER PICTURE HAS EVER BEEN PAINTED WITH SO MUCH... CLAMOR!

Chapter 10

Materials

Artists have painted on all kinds of surfaces with anything that leaves a stain or a mark. In different parts of the world and at different times, people have painted on walls, wood panels, cloth, clay, glass, metal, bark and leather. The materials they used affect how their paintings look.

*Richard II presented to the Virgin and Child
by his Patron Saint John the Baptist and Saints Edward and Edmund*
about 1395–9

Left-hand panel of The Wilton Diptych

A glittering picture

Over 600 years ago, most European paintings were religious. Artists used the most precious materials available, as a way of honoring God.

This golden picture was made for the private prayers of the kneeling king, Richard II of England. It is part of a diptych (a painting made in two panels). You can see the other panel on page 59.

Sparkling gold

The background and the saints' haloes are made of pure gold. Gold coins were hammered into leaf-thin sheets. The gold-leaf squares were stuck in place and polished flat. The background was punched, so that it twinkled in candlelight.

The richly textured gowns were made by scratching a pattern in a top layer of paint. This revealed the gold already put down in a layer underneath.

Homemade paints

Artists could not buy paints ready-made. Their assistants had to make them. Colored earth, metals, precious stones, rocks and plants were ground with water into fine powders. These were mixed with egg yolk into a sticky paste known as egg tempera. The assistants only prepared a small amount at a time and artists had to paint fast, because it dried very quickly.

Painting on panels

Artists painted on wooden panels, sealed with glue and a mixture of chalk and water. Dried and scraped completely flat, these provided a hard, white surface for the tempera and gold. Artists drew their picture in charcoal or ink, and put down any gold before painting in colors.

*The Virgin and Child
with Six Angels and
Two Cherubim*
about 1430

**Attributed to
Francesco di Antonio**

ARTISTS, ASSISTANTS AND APPRENTICES

500 years ago, artists did not work on their own. They were paid to paint everything that needed painting – church and palace walls, furniture and saddles – as well as altarpieces and pictures that could be carried around. They needed assistants to help them. Most artists began as apprentices, at about eleven years old. They learned to draw and to prepare colors. After several years training, they became assistants and helped to paint.

Artist at work

This picture of Saint Luke, the saint of painters, shows how artists worked. It's unlikely they had an ox as a pet, as he did!

The artist painted at an easel. Assistants prepared the paints and put them in mussel shells or pots. The artist put blobs of paint on a palette.

He used brushes made from hog bristles or the hairs of ermine tails, stuck in the hollow quills of bird feathers. He leaned a long maulstick against the picture frame to keep his hand steady when painting fine details.

Saint Luke painting the Virgin and Child about 1530 **Follower of Massys**

Oil painting

Artists in northern Europe discovered a way of mixing colors with oils. Oil paints could be used in thin and translucent layers. The rich, glossy colors were especially good for creating realistic textures and glowing reflections. Since oil paints took longer to dry than tempera, artists could work the paint in different ways. They could also change their designs more easily.

Details

Detail

The Magdalen Reading probably about 1435 **Rogier van der Weyden**

MATERIALS

Painting on canvas

Some artists who used oil paints started painting on canvas instead of on wood. Canvas is a tough cloth that can be rolled up and carried around however large the painting. Canvases were stretched over a wooden frame, like the one shown below. They were sealed with layers of glue and thin paint, so that the oil paints did not soak into the canvas or crack when they dried.

The Stove in the Studio
probably 1865–70
Paul Cézanne

PREPARING COLORS
Oil paints could not be stored for very long. Artists had to decide every day which colors they needed to mix, and how much of them.

Detail

Now you *see* it, now you don't

Early painters liked to show the things
they painted in incredible detail. Later
artists, like Velázquez, used a greater
variety of textures and visible brush strokes.
From afar *(above)*, the king's costume seems
to be embroidered with silver. But close-up *(left)*,
you see only smears, strokes and dabs of gray
and white paint.

Long Grass with Butterflies 1890 **Vincent van Gogh**

Easy squeezy

About a hundred and fifty years ago, factories began making ready-made oil paints in metal tubes. Chemists developed dozens of bright new colors. Now artists no longer needed workshops or assistants for mixing fresh paint. They could have as many colors as they liked, soft and ready for use either indoors or outdoors. They could use these pure colors straight from the tube, just as Van Gogh did (above), or mix them to make other colors.

Broad strokes

New brushes were developed.
They had flat metal holders,
called ferrules. These made it
possible for artists to paint
quickly with broad, flat strokes,
just as Monet did in the picture
below. He painted thick dabs
of green for the trees at the top
left and broken slabs for the
reflections in the water.

Bathers at La Grenouillère
1869
Claude-Oscar Monet

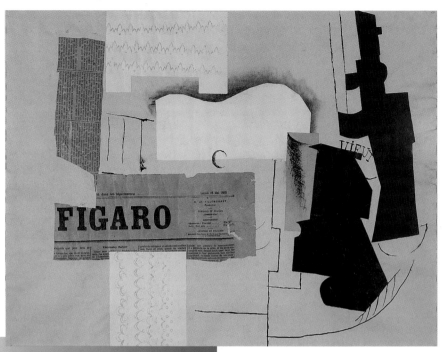

Guitar, Newspaper, Wine Glass and Bottle
1913

Pablo Picasso

Bits and pieces

Early last century, a few painters
began gluing cut-out bits of
newspaper, wallpaper or cloth
on to their paintings. Later, other
artists made entire pictures from
old tickets, newspaper cuttings and
other scraps they found in the street.
This kind of picture is called a collage.

Cut and paste

Matisse made collages with colored paper. Assistants covered huge sheets of paper with paint. Matisse cut them into shapes and arranged them on a background. He described this way of making pictures as "drawing with scissors."

The Snail 1959 **Henri Matisse**

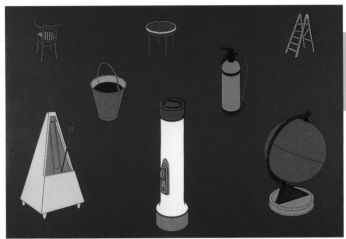

Too many choices

Some modern painters like using acrylic paints instead of oils *(above)*. These can be mixed with water and dry fast. They do not change color or crack with age. Many of the colors are bright and intense.

A gritty mixture

Several other artists have mixed materials, such as earth, straw or dust, into oil paint to give it a new texture.

Dubuffet added grit to paint. He spread the mixture all over

Monsieur Plume with Creases in his Trousers (Portrait of Henri Michaux) 1947

Jean Dubuffet

a canvas and scratched images into it *(above)*. He wanted his paintings to remind people of the graffiti found on city walls.

148

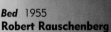

Bed 1955
Robert Rauschenberg

Painting – or the real thing?

Rauschenberg went one step further. He thought that pictures looked more like the real world when real objects were combined with painting.

He wanted this picture of a bed *(left)* to look like a real bed. So he included his actual bedding as part of his painting. He stretched his quilt as if it were a canvas, added his white pillow and painted on both of them.

MICKEY AND DUCCIO'S ARTISTIC OMELETTE

MICKEY AND MINNIE ARE LOOKING AT A PICTURE IN THE NATIONAL GALLERY, PAINTED ABOUT 1315 BY THE ITALIAN ARTIST, DUCCIO. HE WORKED IN SIENA FROM 1278 AND DIED ABOUT 1318. AT THAT TIME, ARTISTS NEEDED ASSISTANTS TO MAKE PAINTS BY GRINDING COLORS WITH WATER AND EGG.

"DID YOU KNOW, MINNIE? ONE OF MY ANCESTORS WAS DUCCIO'S APPRENTICE... AND HE MADE A GREAT DISCOVERY!

REALLY? TELL ME ABOUT IT!

YOUNG MICHELOZZO WENT TO DUCCIO TO LEARN ABOUT PAINTING...

YOU'RE IN LUCK. ONE OF MY APPRENTICES IS SICK, SO I NEED AN EXTRA PAIR OF HANDS!

AS YOU CAN SEE, MY WORKSHOP IS VERY BUSY. I'VE GOT AN IMPORTANT COMMISSION FROM THE CARDINAL OF OSTIA...

... FOR A PORTABLE ALTARPIECE!

MASTER, THE GOLD LEAF HAS ALMOST RUN OUT!

LEAVE IT TO ME! I'LL TAKE SOME GOLD COINS TO THE GOLD BEATER.

WHAT ABOUT ME, MASTER?

YOU CAN FETCH SOME EGGS FROM THE FARM!

??

YOU KNOW WHAT TO DO WITH THEM, DON'T YOU?

UHH ... YES!

SO ...

HERE THEY ARE! NEW-LAID, JUST AS MASTER DUCCIO LIKES THEM! MAKE GOOD USE OF THEM!

YOU BET!

I DIDN'T THINK AN ARTIST'S APPRENTICE HAD TO MAKE LUNCH ... BUT I'LL PUT IN ALL THE ART I CAN!

IN FACT...

A MASTERPIECE, MY LAD! AS A COOK, YOU'RE A REAL ARTIST!

HEE, HEE!

AND NOW LET'S SEE IF YOU CAN MAKE THE PAINTS JUST AS WELL!

PAINTS? WHAT PAINTS?

THE ONES YOU'RE GOING TO MAKE WITH THE EGGS YOU BOUGHT.

OH NO! I USED THEM ALL FOR THE OMELETTE!

HA! HA! HA! HA!

I FORGIVE YOU! BUT YOU'D BETTER RUSH BACK TO THE FARM AND GET SOME MORE, OTHERWISE WE CAN'T GET ON WITH OUR WORK!

HERE YOU ARE, MASTER!

WELL, GET GRINDING, MY BOY!

THIS IS VERY STRANGE...

...I'VE NEVER SEEN SUCH A PALE PINK!

ER, UM... I THINK IT MUST BE THE EGGS.

I BOUGHT THEM IN TOWN TO SAVE TIME ...AND THEY HAVE MUCH PALER YOLKS THAN COUNTRY EGGS!

THAT MUST BE IT!

I'M SORRY, MASTER! I'VE MADE A MESS OF THINGS AGAIN!

NOT AT ALL! THANKS TO YOU, I'VE MADE AN AMAZING DISCOVERY!

THIS COLOR IS PERFECT FOR THE BABY'S DELICATE SKIN!

OH! SO CAN I STAY AS YOUR APPRENTICE?

YES... BUT NOT AS AN APPRENTICE PAINTER! I'VE THOUGHT OF SOMETHING FAR MORE SUITABLE!

WHAT WAS THAT?

DUCCIO HIRED MICHELOZZO AS AN APPRENTICE COOK!

Looking at
Paintings

A LL THE PICTURES in this book are merely reproductions. It is as if you'd been looking at photos of your family and friends in an album, instead of meeting them face to face. What's more, many of the paintings have been shrunk or enlarged to fit the size of the book.

Those that look small on the page may, in fact, be huge, but you can't be overwhelmed by their size. Nor can you be amazed at the magic of a scene that appears vast in the book, but in reality is no bigger than a hand mirror. The "real gold leaf" and the "paint" are only printer's ink, so you can't see how thick, or slick, the texture is and the colors may not be exactly true.

Cognoscenti in a Room hung with Pictures about 1620 **Flemish**

But if you go to a gallery – like the National Gallery in London where most of these are on show – you can look at original paintings. Don't try to see them all at one time; it's too exhausting! Find a few, take your time to look at them from a distance. Then move closer and engage them in silent conversation through your eyes, remembering what you have read. You can be sure they will respond.

Art Words

Below are explanations of some words
that people often use when talking or writing about painting. Look
up the listed pages to see examples of pictures
relevant to each explanation.

abstract painting
A picture that has no subject other than lines, shapes and colors (see pages **35** and **47**).

altarpiece
A painting set behind, or above, the altar table in a Christian church, to help people focus their prayers (see pages **99** and **119**).

composition
The arrangement of all parts of a painting into a satisfactory whole.

easel painting
A portable picture, which has been painted propped on an easel (see page **140**).

foreshortening
A way of drawing objects so that they appear to go back into a painting, instead of lying flat across its surface (see page **22**).

illustration
A picture that decorates or shows an event in a story or explains something in a piece of writing.

Impressionists
A group of painters working in France from about 1870 to the early 1900s. They believed that painting should record only what an artist can see: the bustle and energy of modern life and the changing effects of light and movement.

Impressionist artists include Monet (see pages **20**, **58** and **145**), Renoir (see page **62**) and Pissarro (see page **71**).

landscape
A painting recording a real or imaginary outdoor view (see e.g. pages **64**, **75**, **84** and **144**). There are also seascapes (see e.g. pages **112/3** and townscapes (see page **89**).

Old Masters
A phrase used for famous Western artists who lived in the past and whose work is now in a gallery or museum (e.g. pages **13**, **45**, **118** and **143**).

mural
A large picture either painted directly on a wall or wall-sized (see page **22**, bottom).

patron
Someone who pays an artist to make a work of art especially for him or her (see pages **14**, **17**, bottom and **21**), or who supports artists by buying their work.

portrait
A picture which records the appearance, character and, perhaps, the social standing of a particular person (see pages **12**, **16**, **17**, **32**, **33**, **45** and **125**).

self portrait
A portrait that an artist makes of him or herself (see pages **12** and **103**, top).

sketch
A rapid record of what things look like or a composition, often done in preparation for a painting.

still life
A picture that focuses on objects that don't move, such as food, flowers, pottery or musical instruments (see pages **25**, **36**, **61**, **74** and **91**).

studio
The place where an artist keeps his equipment and does his work, either alone or with assistants. See also workshop.

style
The look of paintings typical of either a particular artist or period. An artist's style is one that is recognizable as his or her own (see e.g. page **143**).

symbol
Something in a painting that stands for something else. A daisy, for example, was sometimes painted as a symbol of innocence.

workshop
The word for an artist's studio before about 1600, when artists still prepared their own paints.

Picture List

All the pictures in this book are from the National Gallery, London,
and painted in oil on canvas, unless otherwise stated.

Page 12 Giovanni Battista Moroni, 1520/4–1578, *Portrait of a Gentleman*, 185.4 x 99.7 cm.
Elizabeth Louise Vigée Le Brun, 1755–1842, *Self Portrait in a Straw Hat*, 97.8 x 70.5 cm.
Page 13 Diego Velázquez, 1599–1660, *Las Meninas*, 317.5 x 276.86 cm. Madrid, Museo Nacional del Prado. © Museo Nacional del Prado. Madrid.
Page 14 Thomas Gainsborough, 1764–1842, *Mr and Mrs William Hallett*, 236.2 x 179.1 cm.
Page 15 Gerard ter Borch, 1617–1681, *The Swearing of the Oath of Ratification of the Treaty of Münster*, 45.4 x 58.5 cm. Oil on copper.
Page 16 Emile-Jean-Horace Vernet, 1789–1863, *The Emperor Napoleon*, 72.4 x 59.7 cm.
Page 17 Gustave Moreau, 1826–1898, *Saint George and the Dragon*, 141 x 96.5 cm. Anthony van Dyck, 1599–1641, *Equestrian Portrait of Charles I*, 365 x 292.1 cm.
Page 18 Pieter de Hooch, 1629–1684, *The Courtyard of a House in Delft*, 73.5 x 60 cm. Nicolaes Maes, 1634–1693, *A Woman scraping Parsnips, with a Child standing by her*, 35.6 x 29.8 cm. Oil on oak.
Page 19 Marinus van Reymerswaele, active 1509?, died after 1567, *Two Tax Gatherers*, 92.1 x 74.3 cm. Oil on oak. Sassoferrato, 1609–1685, *The Virgin in Prayer*, 73 x 57.7 cm.
Page 20 Hilaire-Germain-Edgar Degas, 1834–1917, *Beach Scene*, 47 x 82.6 cm. Oil on paper, three pieces, mounted on canvas. Aelbert Cuyp, 1620–1691, *Ubbergen Castle*, 32.1 x 54.5 cm. Oil on oak. Thomas Jones, 1742–1803, *A Wall in Naples*, 11.4 x 15.9 cm. Oil on paper, laid down on canvas. Claude-Oscar Monet, 1840–1926, *Lavacourt under Snow*, 59.7 x 80.6 cm. © ADAGP, Paris and DACS, London 2002. Christoffer Wilhelm Eckersberg, 1783–1853, *View of the Forum in Rome*, 32 x 41 cm.
Page 21 Bartolomé Bermejo, documented 1468–1495, *Saint Michael triumphant over the Devil with the Donor Antonio Juan*, 179.7 x 81.9 cm. Oil and gold on wood.
Page 22 Sassetta, 1392?–1450, *The Legend of the Wolf of Gubbio*, 86.5 x 52 cm. Tempera on poplar. Luca Giordano, 1634–1705, *Perseus turning Phineas and his Followers to Stone*, 285 x 366 cm.
Page 23 Pablo Picasso, 1881–1973, *Guernica*, 349.3 x 776.6 cm. Madrid, Museo Nacional Centro de Arte Reina Sofía © Succession Picasso/DACS, London 2002. Photo: Museo Nacional Centro de Arte Reina Sofía Photographic Archive, Madrid.
Page 24 Paolo Uccello, 1397–1475, *The Battle of San Romano*, 182 x 320 cm. Tempera on poplar.
Page 25 Jan van Huysum, 1682–1749, *Flowers in a Terracotta Vase*,133.5 x 91.5 cm.
Page 32 Jacob Jordaens, 1593–1678, *Portrait of Govaert van Surpele(?) and his Wife*, 213.3 x 189 cm.
Page 33 Anthony van Dyck, 1599–1641, *Portrait of Cornelis van der Geest*, 37.5 x 32.5 cm. Oil on oak.
Page 35 Jackson Pollock, 1912–1956, *Number 3, 1949: Tiger*, 157.7 x 94.6 cm. Oil, enamel, metallic enamel, string, and cigarette fragment on canvas mounted on fibreboard. Hirshhorn Museum and Sculpture Garden, Smithsonian Institution, Gift of Joseph H. Hirshhorn, 1972 (72.235) © ARS, NY

and DACS, London 2002. Photo: Hirshhorn Museum and Sculpture Garden, Smithsonian Institution.
Page 36 Luis Meléndez, 1716–1780, *Still Life with Oranges and Walnuts*, 61 x 81.3 cm.
Page 37 Pieter Saenredam, 1597–1665, *The Interior of the Grote Kerk at Haarlem*, 59.5 x 81.7 cm. Oil on oak.
Page 38 Workshop of Robert Campin (Jacques Daret?), 1378/9–1444, *Virgin and Child in an Interior*, 18.7 x 11.6 cm. Oil on oak. William Charles Ross, 1794–1860, *Prince Albert*, 5.5 x 4.5 cm. Watercolor on ivory. Follower of Hugo van der Goes, *The Virgin and Child*, 32.3 x 21.4 cm. Oil on oak.
Page 39 Francesco Guardi, 1712–1793, *Caprice View with Ruins*, 10.1 x 6.1 cm. Oil on wood.
Pages 41, 47 Frank Stella, born 1936, *Ophir*, 250.19 x 210.19 cm. Copper paint on canvas. Private Collection © ARS, NY and DACS, London 2002. Photo: Courtesy of Leo Castelli Gallery, New York.
Page 42 Cave paintings at Lascaux, France, Perigeux, Centre National de Prehistoire, Lascaux Cave, Salle des Taureaux, © C.N.P. Ministère de la Culture, France. Photo: N. Aujoulat.
Pages 43, 48 Lysippides, active 530–510 BC, *Storage jar (amphora) showing Ajax and Achilles playing a game resembling backgammon*. The British Museum, London. © Copyright The British Museum.
Page 44 Sandro Botticelli, about 1445–1510, *Venus and Mars*, 69.2 x 173.4 cm. Oil and tempera on poplar.
Page 45 Hans Holbein the Younger, 1497/8–1543, *Christina of Denmark, Duchess of Milan*, 179.1 x 82.6 cm. Oil on oak.
Page 46 Sandro Botticelli, 1445–1510, *The Adoration of the Kings*, Diameter 130.8 cm. Tempera on poplar.
Page 56 Jan van Os, 1744–1808, *Fruit and Flowers in a Terracotta Vase*, 89.1 x 71 cm. Oil on mahogany.
Page 57 Jean-Auguste-Dominique Ingres, 1780–1867, *Madame Moitessier*, 120 x 92.1 cm.
Page 58 Claude-Oscar Monet, 1840–1926, *The Water-Lily Pond*, 88.3 x 93.1 cm. © ADAGP, Paris and DACS, London 2002.
Page 59 English or French, unknown artist, 14th century, *Right-hand panel of The Wilton Diptych*, 57 x 29.2 cm. Egg tempera on oak.
Page 60 Hilaire-Germain-Edgar Degas, 1834–1917, *Combing the Hair*, 114.3 x 146.1 cm.
Page 61 Vincent van Gogh, 1853–1890, *Sunflowers*, 92.1 x 73 cm.
Page 62 Pierre-Auguste Renoir, 1841–1919, *Boating on the Seine*, 71 x 92 cm.
Page 64 John Constable, 1776–1837, *The Cornfield*, 142.9 x 121.9 cm.
Page 65 Herman Saftleven,1609–1685, *Christ teaching from Saint Peter's Boat on the Lake of Gennesaret*, 46.7 x 62.8 cm. Oil on oak.
Page 68 Geertgen tot Sint Jans, about 1455/65– about 1485/95, *The Nativity, at Night*, 34.3 x 25.1 cm. Oil on oak.
Page 70 Jean-Baptiste-Camille Corot, 1796–1875, *Peasants under the Trees at Dawn*, 28.2 x 39.7 cm.
Page 71 Camille Pissarro, 1830–1903, *The Boulevard Montmartre at Night*, 53.3 x 64.8 cm.
Page 72 Follower of Rembrandt, *A Man seated reading at a Table in a Lofty Room*, 55.1 x 46.5 cm. Oil on oak.
Page 73 René Magritte, 1898–1967, *Empire of Lights*,

50 x 60 cm. Private Collection © ADAGP, Paris and DACS, London 2002. Photo: Bridgeman Art Library, London.
Page 74 Jan Jansz. Treck, 1605/6–1652, *Still Life with a Pewter Flagon and two Ming Bowls*, 76.5 x 63.8 cm.
Page 75 Henri Matisse, 1912–13, *Landscape viewed from a Window*, 115cm x 80 cm. Moscow, Pushkin Academy. © Succession H Matisse/DACS 2002. Photo: SCALA, Florence.
Pages 78, 81 Claude-Oscar Monet, 1840–1926, *The Gare St-Lazare*, 54.3 x 73.6 cm. © ADAGP, Paris and DACS, London 2002.
Page 84 Pierre-Etienne Théodore Rousseau, 1812–1867, *The Valley of St. Vincent*, 18 x 34.9 cm. Oil on paper, laid down on canvas.
Page 85 Eugène Boudin, 1824–1898, *The Beach at Tourgéville-les-Sablons*, 50.8 x 74.3 cm.
Page 86 Meindert Hobbema, 1638–1709, *The Avenue at Middelharnis*, 103.5 x 141 cm.
Page 88 Gerrit Berckheyde, 1638–1698, *The Market Place and the Grote Kerk at Haarlem*, 51.8 x 67 cm.
Page 89 Canaletto, 1697–1768, *Venice, Piazza San Marco*, 46.4 x 37.8 cm.
Page 90 Hilaire-Germain-Edgar Degas, 1834–1917, *Miss La La at the Cirque Fernando*, 116.8 x 77.5 cm.
Page 91 Vincent van Gogh, 1853–1890, *Van Gogh's Chair*, 91.8 x 73 cm.
Page 92 From a tomb in Thebes, *Ornamental Fishpond in the Garden of Nebamum*, Height 64 cm. Wall painting, paint on plaster. The British Museum, London. © Copyright The British Museum, London
Page 93 Ch'iu Ying, 1510–1551, *The Emperor Guang-wu Fording a River*, 170.8 x 65.4 cm. Scroll: ink and color on silk. Ottawa, National Gallery of Canada. © Ottawa, National Gallery of Canada. Purchased, 1956.
Page 94 Hendrick ter Brugghen, 1588?–1629, *The Concert*, 99.1 x 116.8 cm.
Page 95 Marc Chagall, 1887–1985, *I and the Village*, 192.1 x 151.4 cm. New York, The Museum of Modern Art (Mrs Simon Guggenheim Fund) © ADAGP, Paris and DACS, London 2002. Photo: The Museum of Modern Art, New York.
Page 99 Carlo Crivelli, 1430/5–about 1494, *The Annunciation, with Saint Emidius*, 207 x 146.7 cm. Egg and oil on canvas, transferred from wood.
Page 100 Antonello da Messina, active 1456, died 1479, *Saint Jerome in his Study*, 45.7 x 36.2 cm. Oil on lime.
Page 102 Frans Hals, 1580?–1666, *Portrait of a Woman (Marie Larp?)*, 83.4 x 68.1 cm.
Page 103 Bartolomé Esteban Murillo, 1617–1682, *Self Portrait*, 122 x 107 cm. Jan Gossaert, active 1503, died 1532, *A Little Girl*, 38.1 x 28.9 cm. Oil on oak.
Page 106 Leonardo da Vinci, 1452–1519 *Portrait of Mona Lisa*, 70 x 53 cm. Wood panel. Musée du Louvre, Paris. © Photo RMN. Photo: R.G. Ojeda.
Page 112 Willem van de Velde the Younger, 1633–1707, *Dutch Ships in a Calm*, 35.7 x 43.3 cm. Oil on wood. Studio of Willem van de Velde, *Small Dutch Vessels in a Breeze*, 21 x 29.6 cm. Oil on oak.
Page 114 Joseph Mallord William Turner, 1775–1851, *Rain, Steam, and Speed – The Great Western Railway*, 90.8 x 121.9 cm.
Page 115 Henri Rousseau, 1844–1910, *Tiger in a Tropical Storm (Surprised!)*, 129.8 x 161.9 cm.
Pages 116, 129 (detail) Giacomo Balla, 1871–1958, *Dynamism of a Dog on a Leash*, 90.17 x 109.86 cm. Collection Albright-Knox Art Gallery Buffalo, New York.

Bequest of A. Cinger Goodyear and Gift of George F. Goodyear, 1964. © DACS, London 2002. Photo: Albright-Knox Art Gallery Buffalo, New York.
Page 117 Victor Vasarely, 1908–1997, *Supernovae*, 241.9 x 152.4 cm. Tate, London. © ADAGP, Paris and DACS, London 2002.
Page 118 Jan Vermeer, 1632–1675, *A Young Woman standing at a Virginal*, 51.7 x 45.2 cm.
Page 119 Piero della Francesca, about 1415/20–1492, *The Baptism of Christ*, 167 x 116 cm. Egg on poplar.
Page 122 Titian, active about 1506, died 1576, *Bacchus and Ariadne*, 175.2 x 190.5 cm.
Page 124 Charles Demuth, 1883–1935, *I Saw the Figure 5 in Gold*, 91.44 x 75.57 cm. Oil on board. New York, The Metropolitan Museum of Art. Alfred Stieglitz Collection, 1949. (49.59.1) Photograph © 1986 The Metropolitan Museum of Art, New York.
Page 125 Sir Joshua Reynolds, 1723–1792, *Colonel Banastre Tarleton*, 236.2 x 145.4 cm.
Page 126 Jean-Siméon Chardin, 1699–1779, *The House of Cards*, 60.3 x 71.8 cm.
Page 127 Caspar David Friedrich, 1774–1840, *Winter Landscape*, 32.5 x 45 cm.
Page 136 English or French, unknown artist, 14th century, Left-hand panel of *The Wilton Diptych*, 57 x 29.2 cm. Egg tempera on oak.
Page 138 Attributed to Francesco di Antonio, active 1393–1433 (or later), *The Virgin and Child with Six Angels and Two Cherubim*, 85 x 54 cm. Tempera on wood.
Page 140 Follower of Massys, *Saint Luke painting the Virgin and Child*, 113.7 x 34.9 cm. Oil on oak.
Page 141 Rogier van der Weyden, about 1399–1464, *The Magdalen Reading*, painted surface 61.6 x 54.6 cm. Oil on mahogany, transferred from another panel.
Page 142 Paul Cézanne, 1839–1906, *The Stove in the Studio*, 41 x 30 cm.
Page 143 Diego Velázquez, 1599–1660, *Philip IV of Spain in Brown and Silver*, 195 x 110 cm.
Page 144 Vincent van Gogh, 1853–1890, *Long Grass with Butterflies*, 64.5 x 80.7 cm.
Page 145 Claude-Oscar Monet, 1840–1926, *Bathers at La Grenouillère*, 73 x 92 cm. © ADAGP, Paris and DACS, London 2002.
Page 146 Pablo Picasso, 1881–1973, *Bottle of Vieux Marc, Glass, Guitar and Newspaper*, 46.7 x 62.5 cm. Collage and pen and ink on blue paper. Tate, London © Succession Picasso/DACS, London 2002. Photo: Tate, London 2002.
Page 147 Henri Matisse, 1869–1954, *The Snail*, 286.4 x 287 cm. Gouache on paper, cut and pasted on paper mounted on canvas. Tate, London © Succession H Matisse/DACS 2002. Photo: Tate, London 2002.
Page 148 Jean Dubuffet, 1901–1985, *Monsieur Plume with Creases in his Trousers (Portrait of Henri Michaux)*, 130.2 x 96.5 cm. Oil and grit on canvas. Tate, London © ADAGP, Paris and DACS, London 2002. Photo: Tate, London. Michael Craig-Martin, born 1941, *Knowing*, 244.2 x 366.5 cm. Acrylic on canvas. Tate, London © Michael Craig-Martin. Courtesy of Waddington Galleries, London. Photo: Tate 2002.
Page 149 Robert Rauschenberg, born 1925, *Bed*, 191.14 x 80.01 x 15.88 cm. Combine painting. New York, Collection of Mr. & Mrs. Leo Castelli © Untitled Press, Inc / VAGA, New York / DACS, London 2002. Photo: Courtesy of Leo Castelli Gallery, New York.
Page 155 Flemish, *Cognoscenti in a Room hung with Pictures*, 95.9 x 123.5 cm. Oil on wood.

First Published by National Gallery Company Limited, 2002
This edition published in 2003 by Bunker Hill Publishing Inc.
26 Adams Street, Charlestown, MA 02129 USA

10 9 8 7 6 5 4 3 2

Library of Congress Cataloging in Publication Data available from the publisher's offoce

ISBN 1 59373 008 X

Printed in China by Jade Productions